The Whispering Willow

by
Judy Barnes

BLUEPRINT PRESS
INTERNATIONALE

The Whispering Willow

ISBN
978-1-959365-76-1 (Paperback)
978-1-959365-77-8 (eBook)
978-1-959365-75-4 (Hardcover)

The Whispering Willow

Table of Contents

PREFACE

Who ever heard of a talking tree? Not I. Have you? Someone tells of a Weeping Willow Tree that actually talks to people and tries to give them sage advice about any problem they have. It doesn't matter the age of the person, he talks and makes friends with almost anyone he meets. He is very knowledgeable. No one knows why he is so smart, but he is. He only has one problem. He doesn't know why there are so many holidays. However, he has a good friend who helps him understand the reasoning behind some important days in the year.

As you read this book, maybe you will think about how a tree might want to communicate with people. Maybe he wants to understand the human race. It's a mystery to me.

—Judy Barnes

Chapter One

The phone was ringing. Joanne was eager to speak to Carol.

"Hello?"

"Hello, Carol. I had a super idea."

"Well?"

"Are you busy this morning?"

"Not particularly. Why?"

"I thought it might be fun to take Ronny and Gloria to The Willow Park and have lunch," Joanne said.

"Yes, we could do that. We haven't had a good heart to heart for a long time. I'm sure Ronny would like to go. He hasn't seen Gloria for quite a while," Carol Answered.

"It might be easier to pick up some Happy Meals from Mickey Dees," Joanne suggested. He was asking about Gloria the other day."

"I like that idea better. I'll pick you and Gloria up at 10:00," Carol said.

"Ronny, we are going to The Willow Park this morning with Gloria and her Mom," Joanne stated. "Doesn't that sound like fun?"

"Yay, I love going to the park and play on the slide."

"We are going to a different park today. There's one I'd like to go to. We've never been there before. It will be fun doing something different. I'm sure they will have a slide and other things you and Gloria can play on."

Ten o'clock sharp, Carol and Ronny pulled up in Fisher's driveway. Joanne and Gloria were waiting.

"Get in and buckle up," Carol quipped.

"Hi, Gloria. We are so glad to see you and your mom."

The kids just grinned.

Ronny said, "We are going to a new park today. That will be fun."

"Well, it's new to us. I thought it would be fun to go somewhere different," Carol relayed.

Both kids said, "Yay!"

As they pulled up to a parking space, Gloria complained, "There is a funny looking tree. I don't think I like it. It's ugly."

Joanne explained, "That's called a Weeping Willow."

"Why, is it unhappy?" Ronny asked.

"I don't think so. Maybe it is because of the way the branches hang," was Joanne's only answer she could think of.

Oh well, Ronny seemed satisfied.

As soon as the children were unbuckled and the back doors opened, they ran to the slide. The ladies settled at a near-by picnic table.

The kids ran as fast as they could to see who could get to the ladder of the slide the quickest. They were having a great time.

Then they heard a voice, as soft as whisper say, "Be careful, you don't want to get hurt."

Both of the children looked around, but couldn't see anybody. They ran to their mothers. They looked scared. Gloria said first, "Mommy, I heard a voice whisper to be careful, so we wouldn't get hurt."

Ronny said, "I heard it too."

Carol and Joanne looked around in every direction. There weren't any strangers that they could see.

"It looks safe, go ahead and play."

The ladies started talking. At the same time they were aware of their surroundings. "Joanne, I think Bob is having an affair."

"What makes you think so?" Joanne asked.

Carol continued, "He's been coming home later than usual."

Then they heard a whisper, "Don't jump to conclusions. Give him a chance to explain."

"Where did that come from?" Carol asked.

"That was strange. There's nobody here but us."

"I was going to give you that same answer," Joanne stated.

Carol mentioned, "I feel like someone is listening to our conversation."

Joanne came back with, "That's kinda spooky".

"I know, we better get the kids and leave," Carol suggested.

Joanne nodded in agreement.

Joanne yelled, "Come on kids. We're leaving."

"But we're having fun," Ronny yelled back from the teeter-totter.

Gloria said, "Do we have to? We don't want to go yet."

"Get over here, NOW!" was Joanne's final remark.

Ronny asked, "What's the matter? Did we do something wrong?"

Carol answered, "No, we don't like this park."

Gloria pleaded, "We love this park. There is a lot to do. Can't we stay just a while longer? We were being good."

Joanne said, "Strange things are happening here."

"I didn't see anything bad. We want to stay, don't we, Gloria?"

"Please Mama, can we stay a little bit longer?" Gloria pleaded.

"Ok, but just for a little while," Joanne stated.

Carol gave Joanne a scowling look, "Are you sure we should stay?"

Joanne had a look on her face which indicated she wasn't really sure. But the children were having a good time. Wherever the voice came from seemed to be gone.

"Ok, you may stay for another half hour. Then we will go and get some lunch," Carol agreed.

The children screamed for joy as they ran off to continue playing on the teeter-totter.

Carol and Joanne started where they had left off. "Are you sure that Bob isn't working late?" Joanne asked.

"No, I'm not sure," Carol answered.

"Never jump to conclusions. If he says that is why he is late, trust him. Hopefully he is telling the truth."

Then the Whisperer said, "Sound advice."

Both women looked all around.

"Who said that? Show yourself," Carol said. "This isn't funny. We are having a private conversation. We don't appreciate being interrupted by someone we don't know or who doesn't make himself known to us."

"Look around. What do you see?" The Whisperer asked.

Carol answered, "A slide, teeter-totter, merry-go-round and swings."

The Whisperer said, "I'm disappointed. I'm right here, and yet, you do not see me."

Joanne verified, "There no other people around that we can see."

The Whisperer laughed, "You are correct. There are no other people around."

Carol said, "There must be an intercom somewhere close to us."

Both lady's looked under the table, and under the benches. They looked at the surrounding trees and could find nothing.

"We can't find you. Will you make yourself known to us?" Joanne asked.

The Whisperer answered, "Look straight in front of you."

Carol said, "All I see is a Weeping Willow tree."

"I am the one who is whispering to everyone. I try to guide people when they are heading in the wrong direction," He acknowledged.

"When we were talking about the possibility of Bob being unfaithful to Carol, how did you know how to advise her?"

"Most of the time I just use common sense. For an example, when I told the children to be careful or they might get hurt. You ladies were busy talking to each other and were not watching what was going on with the children. I felt I should intervene and warn the children."

Carol said sadly, "I didn't realize that we were not paying attention to Ronny and Gloria."

Joanne looked down and said, "Neither did I. They are much more important than anything outside of the Willow Park."

"Thank you. From now on, we will pay attention to the reason we are here," Joanne explained.

Then they looked at each other and laughed.

Carol, through the tears from laughing so hard stated to Joanne, "Do you realize we have been talking to a tree? We wouldn't dare tell anyone. They would never believe us and probably call the men in the little white jackets to come and take us away."

Both of the lady's laughed as they walked over to the teeter-totter where Ronny and Gloria were having fun.

George and Harry sat at the table Joanne and Carol just left.

George opened the box he had with him. He smiled and said, "Ready to play?"

Harry returned, "You betcha."

George got the checker board out of the box and laid it on the picnic table. Next he retrieved the red and black checkers, and put them on the board. "Red or black, Harry?"

"You know I always chose black. We've been doing this for five years. You should know by now."

"It's only been three years," George returned.

"I say five," Harry argued.

"Nah, it's only been three," George said.

The Whisperer interrupted, "Would you guys quit arguing? It gets tiresome after a while. You do this every day that you come here."

The men knew The Whisperer by this time. They call him 'The Quiet One'.

"Ok, Quiet One, How long has it been?" Harry asked.

"It's been four years," The Quiet One said.

"No, you're both wrong. I've kept track. It's been five years," Harry interjected.

"That's not important, just play checkers."

Meanwhile, out at the merry-go-round, Joanne and Carol were watching as Ronny and Gloria went around, and around, and around. When the apparatus slowed down, one of the kids would yell, "Make us go fast again".

Joanne would stand on one side and Carol on the other. They would grab it and run as fast as they could while holding onto the merry-go-round. They were having as much fun as the children. Thanks to the Whispering Willow tree.

Behind the Whispering Willow is another bench. Two elderly women sit there often. Their names are Emma and Irene. They are both widows and find comfort in their stories of yesteryear.

Emma said, "It's so good to see you, Irene. How is your family?"

Irene returned with, "Quite well, considering Josephine has cancer in her stomach. She is going through chemo right now, so she is sick to her stomach quite a bit and tired all the time."

"Who is taking care of the family? I know she has several children," Emma recalled.

"Yes, but most of them are grown and are able to help with the

housework. She has a couple of boys that try to take care of the yard, but you know how Josephine always had a beautiful yard. The boys just don't seem to care about it like she did. She never complains, though. I guess she is thankful for what is being done."

Emma asked, "Who does the shopping and cooking?"

"The girls and neighbors." Irene relayed. "By the way, how is Albert doing since his accident? That was so tragic."

Penny takes good care of him. He's home now, although, he is not able to walk yet," Emma announced, and then added, "The worst part is taking care of his bathroom needs. Hospice comes in twice a week and bathes him and changes his bedding."

Irene continued, quietly, "Does he have to use a bedpan?"

"No, actually, he wears adult diapers. Penny changes them several time a day."

Irene stated, "That must be quite a chore."

"Yes, but Penny doesn't seem to mind."

"I hope he gets better soon. Their expenses must be horrendous," Irene said.

"Yes, they are, but he has good insurance from where he works. That is a big load off of their minds. Penny is such an angel. She works day and night to make sure he is comfortable. She has a television close to his bed so he can watch his favorite programs."

The Whisperer yawned loudly and said, "These stories are boring.

I'm going back to listen to George and Harry."

"Good, you do that. We don't like you listening to our conversations anyway."

George was heard to say, “Harry, you’ve cheated again. Every time we play, you cheat.”

“I didn’t cheat, you did. You didn’t crown my king.”

“You didn’t move when you should have,” George announced.

The Quiet One tried to intervene, “I’ve watched both of you, and I’ve seen both of you cheat.”

George stated unfaultable, “I have never cheated in my life. Harry always cheats.”

“Just pick up your checkers and go home. I don’t want to play anymore. And furthermore, I will not be back tomorrow,” Harry said as he stomped away.

The Quiet One said, “He’ll be back.”

George laughed out loud, “I know.” He put the pieces neatly back in the box and strolled home.

The Whisperer said with glee, “Here come Iris and Mandy on their daily jog. I envy them. They always seem so happy. Like they don’t

have a care in the world. It must be great fun to be able to run. If I only had two feet and could run or even walk. Instead I can only stand here in the hot summer sun, or the spring and fall rain. And the snow. How I hate the snow. I get so cold. No one realizes how cold it gets here in the winter. There aren’t many humans coming to the park in the winter. Maybe a few, humans will bring their dogs for a walk. Humans have to be careful walking in the snow. I guess they call it slippery.”

"Hi, Whisperer. I hope you are having a good day," Iris said as she and Mandy hurried past.

"They are such nice girls. Never complaining, always cheerful," The Whisperer acknowledged, If only I could walk."

"Here comes Jenny and Mike. They are in love. They are always holding hands. I was told that when two adult humans hold hands, it means they are in love. Mike even kisses her now and then. That looks like it would be enjoyable. I doubt I will ever know. They talk about getting married. I listen, but I haven't had anything to add. They don't usually argue, but today is different.

"Don't you understand? We have to get married right away," Jenny said loudly, "It won't be very long before I will start to show."

The Whisperer said out loud, "What is going to show?"

"Whisperer, stay out of this. It is no concern of yours," Jenny shouted.

"I thought if I knew what the problem was, maybe I could help," Whisperer returned. The tree really looked as if he were ready to weep. Instead he just pouted.

Then Mike said, in almost a whisper, "Jenny thinks she is pregnant and thinks we should get married. I can't make her understand that we would be making a big mistake."

"Why would getting married be a big mistake? You don't love her? You don't want children?" The tree asked.

"Yes, I love her very much. But I am not ready to get married and start a family. We are both still in college. We don't have jobs or places of our own to live. We can't expect our parents to take care of us and a new baby," Mike explained.

"Whisperer, I love Mike, too. I think we could make a go of it. I think of this sweet baby I might be carrying," Jenny told the tree.

"Why don't you find out if you really are pregnant before you start worrying about what to do?" The Whisperer suggested.

"Whisperer, you are so smart. You always have the right answers to anybody's problem. It is so easy to jump to conclusions. All we need to do is find out if Jenny is pregnant and go on from there. Thank you, friend. We will return in a couple of days". Mike took Jenny's hand and walked away.

"Here comes Dave with his grocery basket. I don't know how he gets so much stuff in it. It looks like he has been dumpster diving again. Here he comes."

"Hi Dave, what new items do you have today?" Whisperer asked.

"Not too much. It has been a bad day for dumpster diving," Dave looked sad. Then he looked back at the tree and smiled, showing the empty places where teeth used to be. "I did find this really nice blanket. It will help keep me warm. You know, winter isn't too far away."

"Don't remind me. I don't think a blanket would do me much good. I get awfully cold."

The Whisperer shivered just thinking about it. "It's still summer so we have a few months before it gets too cold. Say Dave, have you seen your family lately?"

"I sneaked by the house a couple of nights ago, and looked in a couple of windows. My, the kids are sure growing. And they are so good looking. Thank heavens they take after their mother," Dave replied.

The Whisperer's turn, "Have you ever thought of going home?"

"I told you, I went by a couple nights ago," Dave yelled at the Whisperer.

"No, I mean to stay," the tree said.

"No, no way. They don't want me and they don't need me. I would just be a nuisance to them. They seem very happy. I'm sure, I would just make them miserable."

Then Dave looked up and got a faraway look on his face. He was probably remembering the time he spent in Afghanistan while serving in The Army. He had nightmares since his return. At least if he had nightmares while living on the streets, he wouldn't bother anyone.

"I'll see you later, Whisperer, I've talked too much."

"Come again, Dave, when you feel like talking. I'm not going anywhere," the tree teased.

"The sun is going down. I guess it is time for the late afternoon patrons. Yup. Here comes Charlie. He comes the same time every afternoon. I can tell he is getting old. He walks slower and slower each day."

"Hi Charlie, how's it going?"

"Today is not one of my best days. I ache all over. I think fall is coming. I can always tell because of my sciatica. I hate fall and winter. The good thing is, I can look forward to spring and summer."

Charlie smiled as he sat on the closest bench to the talking Willow Tree. "Whisperer, you have it made. All you have to do all day is stand and look at the people then talk to them. People are interesting, and everyone is different. I wish you could help me with my pain. I have so many things I would like to do, but my legs hurt all the time and my walking is getting worse. Some days I don't feel like getting out of bed. I have thought that if I walk more, maybe I could walk better. Not so. The more I walk the more tired I get. Bah!"

"I have never experienced pain, so I don't know how to help people when they come to me with pain. I can help with mental problems, but not physical. I wish I knew what to do or say that would help."

The Whisperer was saddened.

"It helps me just to be able to talk to you and listen to you. You have so much wisdom. More so than anyone else I know," Charlie commented.

"Well, Friend, I must be on my way. I am so slow, it will probably take me a half-hour to get home." Charlie turned and returned the way he came.

It was getting fully dark now. The moon was covered with thick clouds. "There are a few lights in the park, but not in my area. I'm getting cold. Fall is in the air. I'd say it is a little early."

"I see something a little to my right. Oh, that's Peggy out for her nightly jog.

"Hi Peggy, how are you this evening?"

"Hi Whisperer, I'm fine. I'm just getting in my evening run," Peggy remarked.

"Be careful. It's not very safe to jog alone in the dark," came the advice from the tree.

"I'll be fine. I jog every night at this time," the girl said.

Suddenly, The Whisperer said louder than usually, "Peggy be careful, someone is running behind you. I don't like the looks of him."

Then he yelled his loudest, "Get out of here! There are people watching you!"

The man stopped and looked around and asked, "Who's out there? I can't see anyone."

"Leave immediately! This is the police." That was the only comment The Whisperer could think of that might work.

The man turned and ran in the other direction.

Speaking of police, Sergeant O'Malley came strolling through the park.

"Good evening, Mr. Willow. What a grand night. Maybe it will rain. We need a good soaking."

The Whisperer proceeded to tell the officer about the incident with Peggy and the man following her, and how he pretended to be an officer of the law and scared him away.

Sergeant O'Malley listened intently, "I understand why you did that is against the law. Impersonating a policeman is serious.

However, I can just imagine trying to take a tree to the station and booking him for impersonating an officer of the law? That would be humiliating. Just don't ever let that happen again."

He promised Sergeant O'Malley that he wouldn't impersonate a policemen ever again.

The officer left the tree and went to his patrol car.

The Whisperer would try to keep on the lookout for anyone stalking Peggy or anyone else. It's difficult to watch everyone.

Hopefully, everybody is home and in bed. Trees have to get some sleep, too.

The rest of the night was quiet and peaceful.

Chapter Two

"There were rumors going around. George was a few minutes late for his tournament checker game. That is what he called every checker game.

"Hi Harry, where is your partner?"

"Hi Quiet One, I'm sure he will be here soon. Have you heard the news?"

George sniffled, just a bit. "It looks like we'll be losing our park."

"What are you talking about?" The Whisperer asked.

"Yeah, they want to tear up the whole thing and build condominiums. Expensive Condos."

The Quiet One inquired, "What about me?"

"Everything would have to go. All of the swings, slides, merry-go-rounds, teeter-totters, trees; everything!"

Harry arrived and joined in on the conversation. "The children would have to find somewhere else to play. Probably on the streets."

"I haven't any idea where people would go for counseling." George looked down in remorse. "You would get plowed under."

Harry said, "I'm afraid our Quiet One would be six feet under."

George and Harry heard sobbing and turned to see where it was coming from.

Harry remarked, "You really would be a Weeping Willow."

From the Quiet One came, "What can be done?"

"I don't know. It looks hopeless. It will take a lot of people to sign a petition to stop something that big," George added.

Harry said, "Get the checkerboard and checkers out; we might as well entertain ourselves while we can."

George stated, "I don't feel like playing checkers now. I'm too sad."

The Quiet One whispered, "Why don't you boys go to City Hall and get a petition started? That would give you boys something worthwhile to do."

"We better get started. We won't get anything done sitting here."

George and Harry went to City Hall as quickly as they were able.

They entered the large doors and looked puzzled. "Now where?" Both men said at once.

There were about two dozen people standing in different lines waiting to be helped. They looked at different signs to help make things easier for people to get the help each individual needed.

Finally, they both saw a sign that read INFORMATION. "That must be the right place," George acknowledged.

As they were walking slowly to the designated place, two other people got there ahead of the men.

They had to wait, and wait, and wait. Finally, it was their turn. There was a placard in front of the woman that read, MS. JONES. The lady looked nice. She smiled at George and Harry and asked, "May I help you gentlemen?"

George smiled, "Why, yes, you can. We want to get a petition so we can get signatures to keep a park from being torn down."

Ms. Jones took this opportunity to smile. "You will have to go to the PARKS AND RECREATION DEPARTMENT."

Harry moaned, "Another line to stand in."

Ms. Jones stated, "I'm afraid so. Have a great afternoon."

George responded, "You, too."

Harry looked back at Ms. Jones who was pointing in the direction in which the men should go.

This was like the blind leading the blind.

There it was, PARKS AND RECREATION DEPARTMENT. Back in line.

There were probably twenty men in work clothes standing, waiting to talk to the man behind the desk.

"I don't know why they would all be there to get petitions to stop the park from being torn down to put up condominiums," Harry announced for all of the people to hear. There were probably two hundred people waiting in a dozen different lines.

"This is ridiculous. Why are all of these people waiting in all of those lines?" George questioned. "Do you think this is worth it?"

"Think of the Quiet One. He would die. We can't let that happen," his companion said.

Finally, Mr. Petersen said, "Hello, what can I do for you?"

George spoke first, "We're here to get a petition to save our park."

"What is the name of the park and where is it located?" Mr. Petersen looked tired.

"Willow Tree Park. It's located at the corner of Trees and Flowers Streets." Harry rehearsed.

"Oh yes, I know that park well. I've been there many times."

Harry elaborated, "We go there often and play checkers. We argue, sometimes, but all in good fun."

"I understand. I've taken my son, Joey, there many times. We love that park. I can't believe they would tear it down. Do you know what the plans are for that piece of property?"

"Yes, condominiums. Can you believe that?" Harry said disgustedly.

"You can have your petition, and I will be the first to sign it."

George and Harry both laughed and said, "Deal, and we will be the second and third to sign it. That's a good start."

Mr. Petersen retrieved the paper. "You know you have to have two hundred signatures? Or The Man will not even look at it."

George and Harry rushed back to the park. They made a bee-line for their bench. Each person who walked by was asked to sign the petition. Many of them were used to conversing with the Quiet One.

When the Whisperer heard about the park being demolished, all he could do was weep. The branches were touching the ground. If you were very quiet, you could hear his crying, which was just a whisper.

Joanne and Ronny, and Carol and Gloria came to the park to play. The children first stopped at the slide. When they heard the quiet sobbing, they wondered where it was coming from.

Joanne and Carol didn't understand what was going on.

George and Harry saw what was happening. George said, "Haven't you heard what is going to happen to our park?"

Carol responded, "No, we just decided to take our kids here for a couple of hours of fun.

We are hoping they can run off some of their energy. Who is crying?"

"It's a sad story. The Mayor and some of the townspeople want to tear down the park and build condominiums. The Quiet One is sad. He feels that if that happens, he will be cut down."

Joanne asked, "Who is the Quiet One?"

Harry answered, "See that Weeping Willow tree over there? He has been crying since he heard the news about the park."

Joanne laughed, "Trees don't have feelings. They don't cry."

"The Quiet One is very much alive and has feelings, like you and I".

Carol looked dubious and remarked, "I'll go see for myself." She walked slowly to the tree. He was sniffling, Carol backed off quickly.

"Joanne, come and see this," Carol beckoned.

By this time, the children were curious. "Mama, what's wrong?"

Joanne joined her friend and children.

"These men are claiming this tree can talk. Have you heard anything about this tree being cut down?" Carol asked.

"Why would they do that, and who is crying?"

"These men say that the park is going to be torn down. And that they will build condominiums in its place," Carol told her friend.

"I don't understand. This is a lovely park. I'm sure they could find property somewhere else. And what does that have to do with whoever is crying?" Joanne asked.

"The Quiet One is crying," Harry interjected.

"Who is the Quiet One? I am confused". Joanne inquired.

It was George's turn, "That tree over there we call The Quiet One. Hasn't he spoken to you?"

"Trees don't talk. Of course, I have not heard him talk," Carol replied.

"Joanne, remember last time we were here? The children heard someone say, 'Be careful so you don't get hurt'. Then we were talking about Bob being unfaithful. Remember someone said, 'Don't jump to conclusions? That must have been The Quiet One."

"I still don't think trees or other plants can speak," Carol added.

"I'm sorry you don't believe in me," The Whisperer spoke amidst his crying.

"Ok, who said that? Don't try to tell me that tree is speaking to me," Carol said.

"Alright, I won't tell you. Let's take the kids and go to the merry-go-round and play," Joanne stated.

"Ok, no more talking trees," Joanne said.

"Ladies, before you go," George begged, "Will you please sign our petition to save our park?"

"Sure, I will sign it. I don't want to lose this beautiful park."

"Thank you, thank you, thank you," repeated George.

"Here comes Emma and Irene," Harry said. "I'm sure they will sign our petition.

Emma asked, "Why aren't you boys playing checkers? It's such a lovely day."

George commented, "Haven't you heard? The Governor wants to tear down our park and build condominiums in its place."

Irene said, "That would be a shame. This is the ideal place to come and bring a nice hot cup of coffee and chat for a while. It's entertaining to watch the children playing on the park equipment. Is there anything we can do?"

Harry answered quickly, "As a matter of fact, there is. Please sign our petition to save the park."

"Gladly," Irene stated.

"Thank you, thank you, thank you," George repeated once again.

The Quiet One seemed to be perking up a little bit.

George and Harry smiled.

"Uh oh, here comes Frankie," Harry lamented. "I doubt he will sign it."

"Hi Frankie, could we talk to you for a minute?" Harry asked.

"No! I don't want to talk to anyone. Leave me alone," Frankie shouted.

"But, Frankie, this is important," George pleaded.

"Nothing is important right now. I have a job interview. If I stop and talk to you, I will be late." Frankie added.

"We understand," Harry related. "Good luck with your interview."

"Hummmph!" Frankie mumbled on his way past.

"I doubt he will find any kind of a job with his attitude. He always seems so grouchy." Harry recalled.

"Here comes Jenny and Mike," the Quiet One said.

"We don't know them," stated George.

"I do," the Quiet One remarked. "They are nice humans, however, they seem to be a little confused."

"They are holding hands. That's a good sign." The Whisperer said.

"Jenny and Mike, come over and talk to me," The Whisperer beckoned.

Before The Whisperer could say anything, Jenny blurted out, "Mike and I are going to get married and we want the ceremony to be performed right here next to you."

"I would love that, but we have a problem. The park might not be here for the wedding. The governor is planning to tear it down and build a condominium."

"They can't do that. Where will we have our wedding? This is the nicest park in the city," Jenny was sobbing.

Mike tried to console his fiancé, "Don't worry, Honey, we'll find another park."

"Absolutely not! There isn't another place I would like us to be married," Jenny said between the tears.

"We have a petition you both can sign to keep our park," George stated.

"Where do we sign? Mike asked.

George handed the petition to Mike and then to Jenny for their signatures. With that done, the couple walked hand in hand with smiles on their faces.

It seemed too quiet for a few moments. Then Dave approached with his shopping cart. "What are you two doing here still?"

Harry looked at Dave and it was all he could do to keep from crying.

"We are sitting here recruiting people to sign the petition to stop the

Governor from building Condominiums on this spot," Harry said.

"Why would the Governor want to do a stupid thing like that?"

"I guess he figures this is a choice piece of property," George said.

Dave continued with, "He must be out of his mind. Yes, this is a great place for a park, not Condominiums. Where will the children play?

Where will you play checkers? Where will friends gather to reminisce? I like to come and dumpster dive. Sometimes I find some pretty good stuff."

"I remember when we were children and we played in this field. We had some great times," Dave looked up and remembered.

"Please sign our petition. Harry and I went to City Hall and got a petition to have citizens sign, so we can try to save our park."

"Gladly, I don't know where else I would go. I've found some of the best stuff in these dumpsters. I remember The Whisperer when he was a sapling. Then I was shipped to Afghanistan. Now look at him, tall and beautiful."

George handed Dave the paper and pen.

"Thank you so much for signing our petition."

Dave said, "I feel like it is my petition, too.

George and Harry stayed until about 10:00. By then they had almost one hundred signatures. Hopefully, they will be able to collect the rest to make up the two hundred names needed to save the tree.

The next day, George was all excited when he reached Harry and The Quiet One.

"I just heard on the news that the Governor is going to have a meeting to show the plans for the new Condominiums next Monday at 10 o'clock in the morning."

"Where is it going to be held?" Harry asked.

"Right here in front of The Quiet One," George announced.

Harry inquired, "What are we going to do? Should we split up and go into stores, and Condominiums?" asked Harry.

George's face lit up like a Christmas tree. "What a splendid idea."

"We might have to go to City Hall and get another petition," Harry smiled.

By the middle of the day, the petition was full. So George and Harry went to City Hall.

Mr. Petersen was behind his desk, "Hi, is your petition filled already?"

"Yes, everyone wants to save Willow Park. We would like another petition."

Mr. Petersen related, "Other people have come in getting petitions."

"Really! Hopefully, we all will make a difference. We've got to save our park."

"We're expecting a crowd on Monday for more than an informational gathering," Mr. Petersen said, "I think it will be a rally. That's what we need," as he got a big smile on his face.

"Here is our first full petition. We're hoping to fill another one, too," George said.

Mr. Petersen handed the men another petition. "Good luck." And he shook their hands.

George and Harry were anxious to get back to gathering signatures.

They had to go together, because they only had one petition.

On Monday, the guys had filled their second petition. They were elated.

At 10:00 a black limousine drove into the parking lot by the park.

Some men carried a model of the new Condominium. It was beautiful; very modern and tall.

There weren't very many people. That was disappointing.

Then Mr. Petersen arrived. And after him, people seemed to come out of the trees. As the people congregated, there was complete silence. Not a cough, sneeze, baby crying, or even a dog barking. It was eerie. The Governor looked nervous.

Governor Jim Cousins started to speak: "Ladies and gentlemen, we are gathered here today to see the new Condominium we propose to be erected on this very spot." He smiled a fake smile and continued, "The first day of next month, everything in this park will be bare. A bulldozer will come in at 7:00 a.m. to demolish everything you now see, and the ground will be as flat as a football field, except no grass." He laughed. No one else was laughing.

One man spoke up, "What about that Willow Tree?"

The Governor smiled, "Of course that will be gone. That unsightly, monstrosity will be gone. Thank God!

"Don't thank God for destroying one of our icons. It has been here ever since the park was erected. Our beloved tree came with Willow Park. You can't just treat him as if he doesn't matter. He does matter."

"Sir, it is just a tree," the Governor stated.

Governor Cousins was starting to sweat profusely. The crowd started whispering. Then it got louder and louder.

Finally, Mr. Petersen handed the Governor six petitions filled with names.

"Sir, we ask you to look at these petitions the City Hall received from these good people. These were signed by the good, upstanding men and women of our community. These people, might I add voters, do not want anything to happen to their iconic edifice."

"So now it is an Iconic Edifice. Maybe we should erect a monument to your Iconic Edifice."

The whole audience raised their arms and cheered. "Yay, build a monument to 'The Quiet One," was heard by the Governor and all of his people he brought with him.

The Governor said, "This is ridiculous," as he wiped his whole face.

The people roared with laughter as they watched the Governor who was overcome with emotions making a fool of himself. He didn't care about the people who came to get the man to change his mind. He cared about the prestige he might lose by going against this large group of people.

He was quiet for a few minutes while he walked in circles wringing his hands. Then he said, "I will go back to my office and think hard about what has happened here today. Then I will make my decision. Oh yes, I will look at all of the petitions and then I will get back to you on the Evening News."

The men took the model and the Governor followed close behind.

The people in the audience were elated. They knew they had won their case.

Chapter Three

Well, you guessed it, Willow Park survived. There were enough signatures on the petitions to satisfy everyone that we didn't need a Condominium where the park now stands. The Governor had to look for a different location to put his high rise. He was not very happy about it, but he had to go along with the majority.

Needless to say, The Quiet One was happy. His home was safe and he felt "Chatty" once again.

The mothers came with their children, George and Harry were playing checkers, the 'older' ladies resumed the gossiping, Jenny and Mike could continuing with the wedding plans.

Speaking of weddings, Jenny and Mikes was coming up very soon. It had been two months since the Condominium Fiasco happened. There were more people and dogs that decided Willow Park was a good place to go. It was convenient for a lot of people. It was always well manicured with beautiful flowers and well-trimmed bushes. Just a lovely place to go to be alone or with someone you love.

Jenny and Mike had sent out invitations, hired a Minister to officiate, and hired a band to play music for the festivities after the legalities were completed.

They had the food catered. There would be roast beef sandwiches on buns, lots of potato salad, chips and salsa, and a beautiful six tier wedding cake. Trash cans were put out for the rubbish. Everything had to be perfect for a Willow Park wedding. The Whisperer had Christmas lights draped on him and he wore them proudly.

They prayed each day before the wedding that the weather would be warm and clear for the proceedings.

The day arrived and Mike showed up wearing jeans and a t-shirt with a tie and tuxedo jacket printed on the front. Jenny wore a white mini dress. I would say that it was very informal. That suited them just fine. The Minister was also wearing jeans and a t-shirt with Church of the Living Christ printed on the front. Not exactly High Class, but it was their wedding and that was the way they wanted it.

Everyone came in their everyday clothes and enjoyed themselves immensely. It was a great wedding. Some people danced, even children. Others sat and chatted or sang if the spirit moved them. It was good clean fun.

A few stayed when most of the others had left to clean up any litter that was left. They wanted to keep the park clean for others to enjoy.

Chapter Four

The weather was getting much cooler. Afterall it was the end of October. Halloween was just a week away. Normally in the fall nothing much happened. People came to the park all bundled up. It felt like it might snow any minute. The Whisperer hated the cold, especially if it was windy. And it usually was. The Park Ranger tried to go along with the seasons. Now was the time for pumpkins and Indian corn and lots of leaves.

Almost all of the trees shed their leaves. What made the leaves most interesting were the variety of colors. Red, yellow, brown, some even green. The Ranger would rake the leaves in a pile. Then the wind would come and scatter them every which way. Or the children that came to the park, would purposefully throw them in the air to see how high they could go.

The Whisperer shivered in the wind. He hated cold weather, but it was inevitable. This was that time of year. The weeping willow also loses its leaves, but it is among the first to leaf out again the following spring. New growth appears in March or April giving the bare branches a green hue. He looks forward to early spring.

"I love to watch the children play in the leaves on the ground. Peter puts them in such neat piles, and then the human offspring spread them all over. That makes me laugh. I have to find things to make me smile or I would get depressed. The humans hear me laugh, but most of the time they do not know that it's me."

"I like to watch weddings. Mike and Jenny's wedding was special. The Minister stood right in front of me. I felt honored to be where I could see and hear everything. The human couple looked so happy. As soon as their baby is born, there will be another human to play in our park."

"Halloween. Peter decorates the park with pumpkins, jack-o-lanterns, and apples for dunking. The children have great fun dunking their heads in the water and try to get an apple out with their teeth. Boy, do they get wet."

"The children have so much fun. They dress in their favorite costumes. Jerry is an astronaut, Adonis is a farmer, Tommy is a scarecrow, and Marianne is a princess. I've noticed that a lot of young girl humans like to be princesses. Joy looks like she is dressed to be a farmer. Hmnm, I guess that is ok. I guess female humans can be farmers too. "

"There are quite a number of children that are dressed up and ready to go Trunk-Or-Treating. If I remember correctly, that is where adult humans bring their cars and park them side-by-side and raise the back end of the cars and display all kinds of goodies. Then the children go to each car and pick out the goodies they want. Yum, sometimes I wish I could go Trunk-Or-Treating with the others."

"Peter does think of me, though. He put orange and black lights on me. I think I look quite festive." The Whisperer smiled in his own way.

"There are games for the young humans and also hay rides.

Usually, around 8:00, parents are taking their younger ones home because there is school tomorrow. That's when the older ones get into mischief. They start destroying jack-o-lanterns and other pumpkins. They have been known to pull on my branches. They are surprised when I whisper 'ouch'. I think it's funny when they turn around looking for who said it. Sometimes that stops the mischief and sometimes they try to get me to whisper to them again."

"Finally, about 10:00 everything is quiet once again."

Chapter Five

"Even though, it is getting colder, humans come to cook out on grills. Some grills are furnished here at the park. Some they bring from home. I enjoy watching the children interacting with each other. The younger usually stay close to the slide or they wait for Mom or Dad to take them to the swings. You can tell by the looks on their faces that they are having great fun."

"Which ever parent stays behind has to fix the steak, hamburgers, and hot dogs on the grill. Quite often it smells so good, I wish I was able to eat with them. I guess I should be thankful I can see and smell and talk."

"There are so many games going on that it's hard to watch them all. Finally, it is getting too cold to have any fun. So everything is packed up and they leave. I'm cold too, but I cannot go anywhere."

"Sergeant O'Malley patrols the park to make sure there aren't any vagrants who try to spend the night here."

The whisperer asked, "How is everything?"

"Pretty quiet, surprisingly enough."

Then a rustle was heard in some bushes.

Sergeant O'Malley put his finger up to his lips, signaling for the Whisperer to refrain from talking. He retrieved his flashlight and headed for some bushes behind the willow tree.

Some kids squealed and ran away quickly. Sergeant O'Malley and the Whisperer laughed. The officer remarked, "I guess I scared them."

The Whisperer said, "I don't think they will bother me for a while. Thank you for your help."

"That's what I'm here for," the officer said as he grinned. "I guess I better be going and make my rounds."

"Good night officer. See you tomorrow," the willow tree said as he let out a large yawn.

The Whisperer shivered in the cool morning air. He said out loud, "It shouldn't be this cold already. It's only the first of November."

"You knew it was coming. Be thankful you still have a home. It was supposed to be leveled off by now," George stated as he sat down on the bench next to the picnic table.

"Where's your friend Harry?" The Quiet One asked.

"I'm sure he will be here soon," George said. "Anything exciting happen around here?"

"Just the same old stuff. When Trunk-Or-Treating was done some kids decided to pull on my limbs. Sergeant O'Malley scared them away. We laughed," The Quiet One related.

George snickered.

“It’s not like Harry to be this late. I wonder...”

The Quiet One asked, “Wonder what?”

“Oh, nothing. I was just thinking. I’m sure he just forgot,” George remarked.

“Maybe you should go and check on him.” The Quiet One was getting concerned.

“I think I will,” the friend replied. “I’ll be back soon.”

George left his box with the checkers in it on the table as he rushed to find Harry.

The Whisperer whispered to himself, ‘I hope Harry is all right’.

A half hour later George returned with his best friend. George had a big grin on his face, “Harry overslept and didn’t get up in time for our game.”

“I’m so glad you are all right, Harry. I was worried about you,” The Quiet One said.

The two men played checkers for several hours. They didn’t accuse each other of cheating. They were just happy to be able to continue to play checkers and be best friends.

For some unknown reason everyone was contented. The park was safe. No one felt threatened. Joanne and Carol brought their children to play on the playground equipment. Emma and Irene came to tell stories about their families.

Iris and Mandy continued with their jogging regimen.

Mike and Jenny returned, holding hands after their honeymoon.

Dave kept coming every evening to check out the dumpsters in the park.

Peggy continued jogging at night. Everything was calm... too calm.

One evening Sergeant O'Malley ran from the parking lot with his gun drawn. No one was within sight besides The Whisperer. All was quiet.

Then Sergeant O'Malley shouted, "Stand still and put your hands in the air".

Rustling was heard in the nearby bushes. No one emerged.

Sergeant O'Malley shouted again, "Come out, now!"

A dark figure came out slowly. He also had a pistol in his left hand, pointed at the officer.

The man shot at the policeman, but missed his target.

Sergeant O'Malley shot his gun and the other man went down.

"I'm wounded, please don't shoot me again."

The Whisperer was too scared to say anything. Nothing had ever happened like this in his park before.

The officer restrained the perpetrator.

The policeman was heard to say on his radio, "This is Officer O'Malley, badge number 2 5 6. I am at Willow Park. I have a young man, eighteen years old, named James Johnson apprehended on suspicion of attempted robbery of a convenience store at Pearl Street and Diamond

Avenue. Please send a back-up patrol unit to escort us to the jail. He is armed and dangerous."

He then turned to the suspect, "Do you live with your parents?"

"No, I have my own apartment," came the answer.

"Why were you trying to rob that store?" asked the officer.

Now the siren was blaring as it reached the parking lot of the park. Two policemen were running to Sergeant O'Malley with their guns ready for action.

The waiting officer said, "I'm glad to see you. I put cuffs on this young man, James Johnson. We have to take him to jail. He was caught attempting to rob the convenience store at Pearl Street and Diamond Avenue."

"Officer, I swear it wasn't me. There was another man buying a pack of cigarettes or so he said.

"What is your name?" the policeman asked.

"Tommy Garcia," the boy answered nervously.

While writing the information in his notebook, Sergeant O'Malley continued with the interrogation, "Do you remember what the other guy looked like?"

Tommy thought a moment before he replied, "Sir, he had black hair about to his shoulders, skin about my color. He had pimples all over his face. He was wearing dirty jeans and t-shirt."

"What about his shoes?" one of the other officers asked.

The boy wracked his brain, "I don't think I even looked at his shoes. I was scared, he had a gun."

"So did you," Officer O'Malley stated.

Tommy pulled his gun from his pocket, "But it's only a water pistol."

"Let me see that," the Sergeant requested. "It sure looked real from the distance between us."

"I don't own a gun. I wouldn't know how to load a real gun. If it was loaded, I wouldn't know how to shoot it," Tommy admitted.

"I need your address and telephone number in case we need you for further interrogation," Sergeant O'Malley said.

Looking at the other policemen O'Malley said, "Thanks for coming. You can get back to your stations now. I'll make out my report and get back to work. Good bye."

"Thank you for not talking while all of this was going on. That would be quite embarrassing," Sergeant O'Malley said.

Chapter Six

"I feel so cold. We had our first snow last night. Brrr. This snow is cold. I wish I had been planted somewhere it is nice and warm all year round. Nothing happens here when it snows."

Just then a snowball hit him right in his mid-section.

The Whisperer said, "Who are you? And why did you hit me with a hard snowball?"

A boy about six years old looked around to see who was talking. "Where are you? I don't see anyone."

The tree continued, "I am speaking to you."

"Are you invisible? Are you a ghost? I can hear you, but I can't see you," the boy said.

"What is your name?" The Whisperer asked.

"I'm not supposed to talk to strangers."

"That's sound advice. I'm not a stranger. I'm a friend," the willow said.

"My name is Jeremy, but I still can't see you."

"Who is your friend? I'm called The Quiet One".

"Billy is my friend. Sometimes he's quiet too."

"Jeremy and Billy, look around very slowly and tell me what you see."

"I don't see nothing."

"Billy, do you see anything?"

Billy just shook his head and frowned.

The Whisperer said, "Look very carefully. You must see something."

"I see a slide covered with snow, some bushes and a funny looking tree."

"I am that funny looking tree. You hit me with your snowball."

"Trees don't talk. Only people talk," Jeremy said.

"I talk to humans that will listen."

"How can you talk? You don't have a face or a mouth."

Billy just nodded in agreement.

Jeremy repeated, "How can you talk?""That's my secret. There aren't many humans that know I can talk. I only speak to special humans. The other ones either make fun of me or don't believe me. I'm usually very careful who I talk to."

Jeremy said, "I won't make fun of you and I'm happy you will talk to us."

Billy just smiled and nodded.

The boys were ready to leave, when Jeremy said, "We will never throw snowballs again."

It was still early morning when George and Harry came calling.

The Quiet One did not talk right away. He didn't know why they would be there without their checkers.

Harry spoke first, "Quiet One, is everything all right? You are being more quiet than usual. George and I thought we would stop by and say hello."

"I'm sorry, some boys were here earlier and had thrown snowballs at me. It made me careful. I don't like to have anything thrown at me. Especially, snowballs. I am already cold. I have nothing to keep me warm. Even my leaves are all gone."

George said, "Stay here. We'll be right back."

"That's silly, where could I go?"

"Ha ha ha," Harry laughed as he followed George to the parking lot. The men returned with a large blanket, which they proceeded to drape over the shivering willow tree.

"How's that, Quiet One?" Harry asked.

"Much better. You guys are the best."

The boys from before, Jeremy and Billy, came back. They brought a friend with them. Skipper, their German Shepherd dog. He looked friendly enough. Then he spied the blanket over The Quiet One. Nobody knows what his motive was, but he grabbed the corner of the blanket and ran.

"I'm cold. Skipper ran off with my blanket."

Jeremy stated, "He just wants to play."

The tree complained, "I don't want to play. I'm trying to stay warm. It's cold out here."

Billy and Jeremy started running in the direction of the dog. "Skipper, Skipper, come back here. You naughty dog. You took the blanket that was keeping the tree warm." The harder the boys ran, the faster the dog ran.

Both of the boys yelled at the same time, "Come back, Skipper."

The dog thought this was an excellent game. He had no intentions of returning.

The boys figured he would go right home. They were right, that's exactly where he went.

He was having a good time. He didn't care if The Quiet One was cold.

Jeremy and Billy reached home right after Skipper. Billy grabbed one corner of the blanket, while Skipper enjoyed pulling on the other corner. It started to tear. Jeremy yelled at the dog, "Let go. We need to take it back to The Quiet One."

Skipper pulled even harder. Billy loosened his grip. Then Skipper loosened his. The boy gently started leading the dog back in the direction of the willow tree. Carefully, Billy guided Skipper to The Quiet One. Jeremy and Billy took the blanket from the dog and put it back on the tree.

Gratefully, the willow tree thanked the boys for bringing the blanket back.

The boys smiled and walked away arm in arm.

Chapter Seven

Christmas was quickly approaching. Each day seemed to be colder and colder. The blanket over The Whisperer was great while it wasn't so cold. However, now he could use several blankets.

"Hi Whisperer," Iris and Mandy said as they jogged by. "I see you still have your nice warm blanket."

"Hi girls. I still have a blanket, but I could sure use some more," the tree related.

"Have a good day. The sun is out, so it doesn't seem as cold," replied the joggers.

"It still seems awfully cold to me. They stay warm because they are running. I am standing still, so along with the wind, I can't get warm. I wish someone would bring me another blanket," he pleaded.

Soon, Joanne and Carol walked by. "Hello, Whisperer, how are you? I see someone brought you a cozy blanket," Carol remarked.

"Hi girls, where are the children?" The Whisperer asked.

"We left them home with their fathers. It's much too cold to bring them with us," Joanne said as they continued their walk. "We'll see you tomorrow, Whisperer," the ladies said in unison.

Next Emma and Irene passed with just a nod. Emma said to Irene, "Look, somebody put a blanket on the willow tree. That was so considerate. Who would have thought of that?" they continued walking.

The tree said in a whisper, "Yes, that was very considerate, but I am still cold."

Dave came with his grocery basket full. He looked at the tree and said to himself, 'the Whisperer looks mighty cold, even with his blanket covering him. I have plenty of blankets. I can give him one'.

Dave reached deep into his basket and pulled out a nice thick blanket and draped it over the shivering tree.

"Thank you, Dave. That helps a lot. I was so cold. How did you know?"

Dave smiled, "You looked cold." Then Dave was on his way to the next dumpster.

Christmas finally came. The Whisperer was sad. He didn't have anyone to spend the day with. Then he heard Christmas Carroll's,

Deck the Halls, Jingle Bells, Frosty the Snowman, etc. That brought his spirits up a lot. But then he heard Silent Night. He was having his own Silent Night. He was feeling unloved. Nobody came around on Christmas. Everyone was with their families. He didn't have a family.

He continued to enjoy listening to the music. He didn't understand what was happening. The music seemed to be getting closer.

Soon, he was able to see a group of people coming his way. There must be twenty-five or more singing Christmas songs at the top of their voices. He watched as they gathered around him. What are they doing?

As they continued singing, blankets were being put all over his shivering limbs. Suddenly, he wasn't shivering any more. He was covered with blankets. Some were homemade, some were store bought. It didn't matter. He was warm.

Though hard to hear through all of the blankets, The Whisperer said, "I am so grateful for the warmth that was demonstrated here tonight. I'm sure I don't deserve your generosity, but it is much appreciated."

The singing continued as the crowd walked away. They knew they had done something special that Christmas night.

The Weeping Willow actually wept that night, but nobody else knew.

Chapter Eight

The New Year was about to begin. The Whisperer was sad to see the old year end.

"The humans went past me shouting, 'Happy New Year'. I don't understand what that means. Maybe it means that this New Year will be better than the last year. I thought last year was a great year. I met new humans, the park was not demolished and I got some new blankets to keep me warm. Yes, I think last year was a wonderful year."

Sergeant O'Malley stopped by. "I see you have some new blankets."

"Yes, a group of humans came by and gave me enough blankets to keep me warm through the winter months," the tree announced.

"That was nice of them," the officer said.

"And they sang songs to me while they were here," The Whisperer revealed.

"Tell me, Sir, how do humans celebrate New Year's? Many have gone by and shouted, 'Happy New Years'. What does that mean?" the inquisitive tree asked.

"It means different things to different people. To some it means a new beginning. That's the way I like to look at it. To others it may have a very different meaning. Mostly, I guess it means a brighter tomorrow. With less violence and more love," the policeman orated.

"I don't know what it would mean to me. Maybe happier humans, more kindness, and humans who are not afraid to show their love and appreciation to others," the Whisperer related.

"What do you mean about humans not being afraid to show their love and appreciation to others?"

"Well, it seems like I see a lot of humans who are mad at each other and argue and yell at each other," the tree expressed. "I would like to see more love and understanding."

"I agree with you, but as long as there are different opinions, there will be arguments and discord. If you can help change that, more power to you." Officer O'Malley.

The Whisperer stated, "I listen to them all and try to give little bit of wisdom where I can."

"And from what I can see, you are doing a splendid job."

If the Whisperer could blush, this would be the time.

"Some people make resolutions stating how they would like to change in the coming year. For example, some might want to lose weight, some might want to gain weight, some might want to change the way they talk, maybe clean up their language, some might actually want to be kinder.

There are many things they can put in their resolutions. But the bad thing is that they sometimes forget what they have resolved to do or what not to do the same as this year we are leaving." Officer O'Malley had a big grin on his face. "I'm sure you wouldn't have anything you would like to change."

"Not really," the tree answered. "I hear a lot of singing and shouting, but it seems a long distance away."

Sergeant O'Malley related, "Some people have parties and others go to parties."

"What do they do at those parties?" The Whisperer asked.

"At some, they have games to play, which can be fun. Sometimes they have drinks that they drink to make them feel good."

"Do they actually feel better when drinking?" asked the tree.

"Sometimes, if they don't drink too much. Then they get silly and sometimes even mean. That's when they call me."

The Whisperer asked, "Why do they call you?"

"Sometimes I break up fights and sometimes I have to take someone to jail," the officer said.

"Why do you have to take them to jail? The Whisperer was mesmerized.

"Sometimes the people get so violent, they have to be taken away so they can calm down."

A call came over the police radio, "There's a fight on Mercury Street, in front of 5504 Mercury on the corner of Mercury and James Street. Shots fired. Ambulance enroot."

"Gotta go, Buddy."

The Whisperer thought he heard more shots fired. He hoped Sergeant O'Malley would be safe. He is a good friend.

Soon, everything was quiet once again. Sergeant O'Malley didn't return.

Chapter Nine

Valentine's Day was approaching. The Whisperer was counting on his police friend to tell him about that day. He hadn't seen Sergeant O'Malley since New Year's Eve. Several weeks had gone by. The tree was starting to shed his blankets, one at a time. It was still too cold to take all of them off.

The snow was melting a little each day. Children were starting to play in the park once again.

"I can hear them talking about Valentine's Day. They are mostly talking about what they can get for their mothers."

Suddenly, he heard a voice that sounded familiar. "Sergeant O'Malley, is that you? Where have you been?"

"I'm here, Whisperer. I've been helping people."

"I need help too. My leaves want to grow, but they can't under these blankets. Can you please uncover me?"

"Indeed, I will get you uncovered and give the blankets to some people who can use them." Sergeant O'Malley carefully removed all of the blankets that had kept The Whisperer warm all winter.

"Thank you, you are so kind. It is good to be able to breathe fresh air once again."

"I'm glad I could be of service to you. Now your leaves will be able to grow strong," the officer stated.

The Whisperer asked, "Can you tell me about Valentine's Day? What is it all about?"

"I guess I can explain it according to my own thoughts. I'm not sure where Valentine's Day got its origin, but I have my own feelings. Doris and I have been married twenty years. We love each other very much. So when Valentine's Day comes around we try to do something special for each other. Usually, we go out to a nice restaurant for dinner. And most of the time I bring her a bouquet of red roses."

"Why red roses?" The Whisperer asked.

"Red roses seems to symbolize love," the officer smiled as he answered.

"Oh, I think I understand."

"But then why do young humans celebrate Valentine's Day?" The Whisperer asked.

"That's a good question. They take Valentine's to anyone they like and look forward to receiving some in return," the officer added.

"But, I heard young humans talk about getting something for their Moms."

"I guess some dads allow their children to buy something special for their Moms."

"That makes sense."

Sergeant O'Malley came back later after Googling Valentine's Day on his computer. "I found some facts for you. Every February across the country, candy, flowers and gifts are given between loved ones, all in the name of St. Valentine. But who is this mysterious saint and why do we celebrate this holiday? The history of St. Valentine's.....and its patron saint....is shrouded in mystery. But we do know that February has long been a month of romance. It is believed that St. Valentine's birthday was February 14, so that was the day designated for Valentine's Day. This is a shortened version. It would take too long to tell the whole story."

"That's ok, I was starting to dose off anyway," The Whisperer admitted. However, he perked up when he saw a group of children coming near him. They had their Valentine's with them. They opened them and squealed with each one they opened. The Whisperer decided Valentine's Day was good. The only problem was that they left a mess on the playground.

Sergeant O'Malley was there to make sure the area was cleaned up.

Chapter Ten

"It was St. Patrick's Day. Another holiday? What's with this? It seems like there is a holiday every month. At least it is getting warmer. There is green everywhere.

I'm sure Sergeant O'Malley will be making his rounds soon."

"Hi, friend. Do you know what day this is?" the officer quizzed.

"I heard somewhere that it is St. Patrick's Day, but I don't know what it is about," the tree stated.

"It's a very special day for Irish people. I'm Irish, you know?" O'Malley said.

"Why is it a special day for Irish humans?"

"March 17 is the day traditionally known as the day St. Patrick died. He was the foremost patron saint of Ireland. It was the commemoration of Christianity in Ireland. On that day there are parades, wearing green and shamrocks. Drinking Irish beer and Whiskey."

The Whisperer said, "That is why I've seen so much green today."

"In fact, in some places, if you enter and are not wearing green, you might get pinched."

"Ouch, that wouldn't be nice or fun."

"No, but you don't have to worry, you are always green on St. Patrick's Day."

"Ha ha ha," they both laughed.

That whole day, when The Whisperer saw someone wearing green, he tipped the top of the tree in recognition of the day.

"Spring has arrived. I can feel the warm breeze through my leaves. No more snow. The warmth makes me happy. Young humans are back to playing on the slides, swings, and merry-go-round. Yes, I am happy once again," said The Whispering Willow.

Carol and Joanne were back walking around and admiring the new plants that make the park beautiful.

Carol remarked, "The small plants don't look like much yet, but in another month they will show their beauty."

"Yes, spring is my favorite time of year. We will have to bring our children here on weekends so they can admire the beauty within," was Joanne's come back.

"Whisperer, what do you think of the park this time of year?" Carol asked.

"I love it when I see the humans planting flowers. Then I know how beautiful it will be when the plants get bigger. I love to see it rain.

The warm rain feels so good on my leaves and branches. I love to see the young humans playing on the equipment. They enjoy themselves so much, it makes me smile," he remarked.

"I didn't know you could smile," Joanne said.

"Oh yes, it may not be seen to the outside world, but I smile a lot. I smile when the humans are having a good time. I smile when the sun is warm on me. I smile when it rains. I smile for any number of reasons." The Whisperer related.

"You even smile when it rains?" Carol quizzed.

"Yes, rain brings new life to the park. Everything is green and growing and beautiful."

Joanne marveled, "You have given me a whole new perspective on spring. I always loved spring, but seeing it the way you do, makes me appreciate it even more. I want to go home and plant some flowers so I can take care of them and watch them grow. Thank you, Whisperer."

"Carol, are you coming?" Joanne asked

"No, you go ahead. I think I'll stay here and talk some more to this fascinating tree."

"How old were you when you were planted in this spot?" Carol inquired.

"I think I was about three years old," was the answer.

"How old are you now?" Carol's next question.

"Oh, I'm not sure. Let me think.I must be about eighteen or thereabouts. Why all the questions? I don't know anything for sure," The Whisperer said.

"I'm seriously considering writing a book about you," Carol added.

"I don't think that would be a very interesting book. I'm kind of a dull tree. Have you written any other books? I'm rather boring."

"How can you say that you are boring? How many other trees, or even any plant that can talk?""

"I've never heard any of them, but then I have never tried to talk to them. I only talk to humans."

"Try to talk to other plants," Carol suggested.

"I can't. I'd feel silly," The Whisperer remarked.

Carol said, "Just try. Nobody will see you but me."

"Pretty yellow flower, how are you today? You are beautiful," the timid tree said.

"Do you hear anything?" Carol asked.

The reply was, "No, now I do feel foolish."

"You shouldn't feel foolish. That just proved my point. You are special. You can do something no other Weeping Willow Tree can do. I think it would make a wonderful story for the world to read."

The Whisperer said, "I have an objection to having my story told to the world. I would have humans around me all the time. They would take pictures of me and would touch me and ask me stupid questions."

Carol asked, "What if I wrote it so no one would know where you are? Only your closest friends would know I had written the book about you.'"

"I think that might work," the tree agreed.

"Then that is the way I will write it, and you can proof read it before I have it published."

Chapter Eleven

Carol spent many long days with The Whispering Willow tree. She carried a notebook with her so she wouldn't forget any details. His friends came to visit him often and knew that she was writing a book.

The weather was warmer, however, you have to remember April showers bring May flowers. There were quite a few rainy days. On those wet days, not many people came to the park. Carol didn't come around during the rain. She kept busy organizing the material she already had. May should bring an abundance of beautiful flowers to grace the area.

The days it was not raining the mothers with their children were playing on the play equipment.

Sergeant O'Malley came by. "Hello, Whisperer, how are you doing? I see your friend is here taking notes. Hello Miss Carol."

"Hello, Sergeant O'Malley. Have you been keeping busy?" Carol was interested.

"Just the usual stuff; traffic control, giving tickets to those who think the laws were made for others. It is such a beautiful day, I thought I would stop by and see my old friend."

"You're looking happy today. Sorry, I haven't been around much lately. A man robbed the convenience store last night. He got away with a good amount of money. We caught him as he was coming out of the store. He was just a kid, only fifteen. I don't know what his motive was. I don't know if he was hungry, wanted money for drugs or if he just wanted to see if he could rob someplace. He was taken to jail. I hate to see these young people getting into trouble."

Carol took notes.

The Quiet One was sad, "I wonder if he was one of the little humans who came to play in the park? They have so much fun."

"Yes they do. Maybe if they would spend more time here instead of out on the streets, violence would not be so prevalent."

You could almost see a tear starting to form in the officer's eye.

It was noticed by Carol, how much the man loved his job.

The Weeping Willow was also feeling bad for the boy and also for his friend. "You do the best that you can. You are a wonderful City Servant. I hope the boy gets the help he needs to get back on the straight and narrow. Keep up the good work. Come and see me again soon."

"You can be sure that I will." With that, the officer was on his way patrolling the park as he went.

Carol took notes.

School was out that afternoon, Carol's friend Joanne brought Ronny and Gloria to play.

Carol was so glad to see them, she almost forgot to take notes.

The children had a great time. That was the first time they had been to the park this year.

They literally ran from one item to the next. Around and around they went on the merry-go-round with many others who were enjoying a playtime. Joanne let Ronny and Gloria stay for an hour. That was enough fun for the mother that afternoon. Joanne and the children hugged Carol and waved as they ran to the car. The parking lot was full for the first time in a long while.

Carol took notes.

George and Harry came with their checkers. They were so glad to see The Quiet One that there was no arguing. They played a couple of games and decided it was getting too cool to sit and play checkers. However, they did have a conversation with their friend the tree.

George started, "How are you enjoying this lovely weather? I brought a light sweater in case it cooled down. Now I'm glad I did."

"Yes, it does get chilly, but I'm glad there isn't any snow. That is way too cold," the Willow admitted.

Harry continued, "It's so nice to see the children playing here again."

The Quiet One whispered, "I love the children. They seem so happy and are very inquisitive about me. Most of them have never seen a Weeping Willow Tree. And never one who would talk to them."

Carol could hardly keep up while taking notes. She was learning a lot about what the trees daily life was like. She never dreamed he had so many friends who came and talked to him every day.

There never seemed to be any down time. By the time she went home each evening she was exhausted. She knew she would have enough material for a large book. She spent many hours a week on the computer trying to organize the book.

Chapter Twelve

April showers bring May flowers. How true that is. The Whisperer could smell the fragrance in the air. And the beauty was incomprehensible. He couldn't remember when the park had revealed her loveliness like this before.

Sergeant O'Malley came to visit. "Hello, Whisperer. How are you this beautiful day?"

"I have a question for you. What is Mother's Day? I don't understand. It seems as though there is a holiday for everything."

"I think you are right. How can you have been here so long and you don't know about our holidays?"

"I guess I never thought about it before," answered the tree.

"I don't know the real reason or its origin. The only reason I can think of for having Mother's Day is because she had done so much for us and we love her. She deserves a special day."

"What do you do on this special day?" The Whisperer inquired.

"Some give their mother flowers, candy, or take her out for dinner so she doesn't have to do any work," the officer said.

"What do you do for your mother on Mother's Day?" asked the tree.

"Our family usually brings her a bouquet of spring flowers and then take her to a nice restaurant for a great dinner," the Sergeant replied.

"It's nice to have a great mother and a great son who loves her so much. She must be a wonderful human," the tree added.

"Well, I have to get back to work. Have a great day. I'll see you tomorrow."

Emma and Irene came to visit. Emma related, "I don't think I will be getting anything for Mother's Day."

"Why do you say that?" Irene inquired.

"Penny is getting a divorce and Albert is still recuperating from his accident. They are too busy with their lives to remember me on Mother's Day". Sad, Emma then asked, "What are you doing for Mother's Day?"

"I'm sure I will be fixing a big meal as always," trying not to sound too excited. "The kids will go to church with us and then come to our house."

"Lucky you. Perry and I will probably be alone. I'll fix a small meal for the two of us and then take a nap."

The Whisperer said, "Don't feel sorry for yourself. Make the best of the day for you and Perry. Be happy that you have each other. Hold hands and go for a walk. Come here, we are always open. And it should be peacefully quiet."

Irene interjected, "That sounds like a wonderful idea. Holding hands with the one you love and slowly walking sounds ideal."

"Just because you have a simple meal doesn't mean you have to be glum all day. Make the best with what you have."

"I don't know. I would like to have my whole family over for dinner so it would be special, Emma stated.

"Then after dinner, why don't you and Perry go and visit with Albert and his family for about an hour and then go and visit Penny and her children for an hour. Then everyone will be happy," Irene suggested.

The tree said, "That sounds like a splendid idea."

Emma got a big grin on her face, "I'm sure Perry would like that too. We can go to our children's homes. I will make a luscious dessert to take with us. I can't wait to get home and talk it over with Perry."

Emma and Irene were both satisfied with their plans for Mother's Day.

Carol took more notes. Her hands were starting to ache.

A few days later Sergeant O'Malley came to visit his friend, "How are you doing today?" the officer quizzed.

"I'm doing well. I have talked to several humans about Mother's Day and most have been eager to talk to me. They seem to be excited about remembering their mothers. When they get excited, then I do too. It is so wonderful to discover how much mothers are loved."

Chapter Thirteen

June was a wonderful month. Besides harboring the beginning of summer, it also seemed to be a time for love and weddings.

Sergeant O'Malley came in the middle of the month, "Isn't June great? I think June is my favorite month. Listen to the birds singing their pretty songs, and the bees are busy collecting nectar to make honey and pollenate other plants. Oh, and there is Father's Day."

The Quiet One sighed a loud sigh, "Another holiday?"

"Of course, we can't forget the fathers," O'Malley said.

"Why? What do fathers do? Are they as important as mothers? I'd rather hear about the first day of summer. I'm so happy not to have cold or snow or ice or sleet. I like the warm weather and my pretty green leaves," the tree stated.

"If it weren't for fathers there might be no livelihood. Fathers are supposed to go to work and earn money to pay bills and buy food and clothes and other necessities," the officer relayed to the talkative tree.

"Can't the mothers go to work and pay for the necessities?"

The Sergeant told the Whisperer, "Sometimes that happens. Sometimes the mother has to go to work. Sometimes there isn't a father in the house for a number of reasons. Or if there is a father in the house, maybe something has happened and he is not able to work."

"So Father's Day is celebrated because they are good and take care of their families," the Whisperer told his friend.

"We will leave it at that," the officer said.

"But you are a good father. You take care of your family. You work hard. Being a policeman can't be easy. I know you have been very good to me and our park." The tree signified.

"Thank you, Whisperer. You are a credit to our community," the officer commented.

"You have been coming here for years and I don't even know your first name," the tree stated.

"My name is Norman. You can call me Norm."

"Thank you, Norm. That is a nice strong name. You can call me The Quiet One," the Willow Tree suggested.

You know, you are one of a kind. I'll bet you are the only plant that can talk," Norm injected.

"I don't really know. I've never heard any other plant talk. I tried one time to communicate with a flower, but I didn't get any response.

"Maybe it was shy because you had never addressed it before. Maybe you should try again."

"Maybe," the tree answered. He got up his courage, "Good Morning, Yellow Flower."

They waited a few minutes and then said, "Either she doesn't like me or she doesn't talk."

"I'm thinking, it's the last part. Afterall, who wouldn't like you?"

The Quiet One blushed again. "You are the nicest human I know."

Although, Norm has a family, he considers The Whispering Willow his best friend. Afterall, they don't argue. The Quiet One always asks for Norm's advice or explanations about what different things mean. Yes, The Quiet One is Norm's best friend.

"Norm, what happens in June besides Father's Day?" The Quiet One asked. "I know there are a lot of great fathers, but there must be something else that happens in June. Look at all of the beautiful flowers and fruit. What else?"

"You're right, of course. A lot of couples get married in June. Some of them get married inside of buildings and some get and some get married outside in our beautiful country," Norm said.

The Quiet One thought about that for a while until at last he announced, "That is really nice. Humans can get married whenever and wherever they desire. How wonderful. What kind of buildings do humans get married in?"

Sergeant O'Malley thought a moment, then answered, "They marry in homes, churches. Really, any building that means a lot to them. It really doesn't matter what kind of building as long as that is what they want. Where they get married has to make them happy. It's the same if they decide to get married outside. Whatever makes them happy."

"Is that why Jenny and Mike got married in this park? Did it make them happy?" The Whisperer asked.

"I'm sure that was the reason. They were married where they wanted to be. With all of their friends," Norm answered.

"I wish more humans would be married here. It makes me happy, too," The Quiet One added.

"I think June is my favorite time of the year," The Whisperer stated.

"It definitely is one of my favorite months. Beautiful weather, flowers, green grass. Beautiful green leaves on the trees. Look at you. You are beautiful too," Norm said.

The Quiet One blushed. It wasn't noticeable, but Norm could tell.

Norm admitted, "I have to go. I have rounds that have to be made at certain times. I've spent too much time here now, although, it has been pleasurable. I will be back soon, my friend."

As Norm was leaving, George and Harry arrived with the box of Checkers under George's arm. "How is it going 'Old Friend?" referring to 'The Quiet One'.

"Just fine. Norm just left. It's good to see you," the tree smiled as he spoke to the newly arrived friends.

"We saw him and waved. You have so many good friends. You can always count on us too," Harry mentioned.

"I know, and I feel so blessed," The Whisperer was so happy.

George decided it was time to start the game. He put the box on the table and took the board out and put the checkers in their appropriate places and announced, "Let's play".

The Quiet One enjoyed watching George and Harry playing Checkers and not arguing and yelling. Both won games and were very happy.

While all of this was going on Emma and Irene came to visit The Whisperer.

"Hello, Quiet One. We haven't been around for a while, so we thought we would come for a visit."

"How have you been, ladies?" The Whisperer questioned.

"Emma has a cold. That's why we haven't been around lately. Irene rebutted.

Emma said, "I'm much better now. It's amazing what homemade chicken soup will do for you." She smiled sheepishly at Irene.

The Whisperer saw Iris and Mandy jogging. "Hi girls, how are you two today?"

"Just out for our morning jog. We are fine. Isn't this a lovely day?

How are you? You're looking 'Spiffy' today," Irene remarked.

"Thanks, Irene, I'm feeling well. I feel like I am the only plant that can talk to humans. I feel it is my destiny to talk to humans and maybe I can help them in some small way," The Whisperer said as he smiled.

Irene returned, "I'm sure you help a lot of people. You are not only a therapist, you are also extremely nice. I don't think you have ever had an enemy."

"Thank you, Irene. You are too kind. I have always loved humans. Especially since I found out I could speak their language," The Quiet One admitted.

Carol was still taking notes while wiping away tears of amazement. She never realized she had taking on such a big undertaking.

The Whispering Willow found notoriety in the newspaper after the diabolical article Carol had written and turned into the newspaper after the Governor came away with egg on his face. The Whispering Willow came out looking like the hero, and rightly so.

Carol was given notoriety, she deserved, and was well to becoming the author she had always secretly known she had always wanted down deep. However, she couldn't believe it would be because of a Weeping Willow Tree.

Carol and Joanne remained good friends. Joanne was happy that Carol was famous. She knew no one deserved it more than her best friend who went on to write many more books which brought in a lot of money.

Synopsis

Carol found out Bob wasn't seeing another woman. He was actually working late so he could buy a new car. He wanted to surprise her on her birthday.

George and Harry continued playing checkers every day. They didn't argue anymore. The Quiet One showed them that just playing for fun was much more fun than bickering over who was right and who was wrong. They were a lot more harmonious and easier for The Quiet One to watch and enjoy.

Emma and Irene met every day to talk about their families. They enjoyed the walks around the park and the discussions about Emma's children Albert and Penny.

Albert got better, however, he and Penny were divorced. She had done so much for him, but he didn't understand her devotion. He wanted his freedom. He felt Penny was smothering him.

Penny went to live with Emma. Emma wouldn't admit it, but as she was getting older, Penny's help was much appreciated.

Irene was elated that her daughter, Josephine, made it through chemo and was cancer free. She was home taking care of her family.

Irene found joy in community service. She would take her Irish Setter dog to the hospital twice a week to visit the sick people. Then she would take the dog to a rest home so the people could enjoy her pet. Even with all of that, Irene still found time to go to the park and spend time with her good friend Emma.

Iris and Mandy didn't jog anymore. Mandy had sciatica and it hurt to run. She had to use a walker, so she and Iris would go to the park to talk with The Whispering Willow. They had some enlightening conversations.

Jenny and Mike had a baby girl they named Olive after her mother. They went to the park often to walk around with Olive and enjoyed the flora and fauna.

Peter, the gardener, took great care of the landscape at the park.

People came from all over the city to congratulate The Whispering Willow for the good that he is able to accomplish and to hear him talk. It is still hard to believe that a tree can actually hold conversations with people.

They also come for advice on any numbers of subjects. They all were amazed at the knowledge of a tree. Where did he obtain such understanding of life and how humans should treat one another? His philosophy is the old time Golden Rule: Treat each other like you would like to be treated. He feels like that is the only way humans will get along in the world...

If you are ever around Tree and Flower Streets, visit Willow Tree Park. Stop and talk to the Whispering Willow. I'm sure you would have a good time.

www.ingramcontent.com/pod-product-compliance
Lightning Source LLC
Chambersburg PA
CBHW051644120626
46551CB00015B/2205
* 9 7 8 1 9 5 9 3 6 5 7 6 1 *